Explore a Spooky Swamp

A bullfrog pokes its head
out of the water in a swamp.

By Wendy W. Cortesi
Photographs by Joseph H. Bailey

☐ BOOKS FOR YOUNG EXPLORERS
☐ NATIONAL GEOGRAPHIC SOCIETY

Willie and Isabella are ready for a new adventure.
They are going to explore the Okefenokee Swamp
with a guide named Johnny.
Boots will protect their feet when they get out of the boat.
Off they go! Johnny pushes the boat forward with a long pole.
On the way, he tells the children about the swamp.
In a swamp, shallow water covers almost all the land,
but trees and other plants grow in the water.
This swamp also has islands, where the land is dry and firm.
The children wonder what kinds of animals they will find.

They have come to an open place without any trees.
Johnny shows the children where to find some tiny frogs.
They are sitting on the green lily pads in the water.
"I've got one," says Isabella.
The children are careful not to hurt the frogs.
In a few minutes, they put them back on their lily pads.

This frog
is even smaller
than
Willie's thumb.

SNAPPING TURTLE

The snapping turtle has
a sharp, pointed beak.
If it is hungry or disturbed,
it will snap
at whatever moves nearby.

AMERICAN ALLIGATOR

With jaws wide open, this mother alligator is defending her nest.
First the mother lays her eggs.
Then she covers them with grass and leaves.
When the eggs hatch, the baby alligators make grunting sounds.
This tells the mother to uncover her babies.

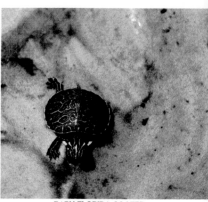

BABY FLORIDA COOTER

GLASS LIZARD

$\mathcal{J}$ohnny reminds the children to watch carefully. They might see a furry otter with a fish. Otters dive underwater to find their food. The cooter is a turtle that lives in the quiet waters of the swamp. The glass lizard looks like a snake because it has no legs.

Which one is stronger?
When two male deer fight,
they lower their heads
and charge.
They push against each other
with their heads
and their curved antlers.
The fight usually ends
when one of the deer gets tired
and runs away.

The deer live
near the edge of the swamp
and on the islands,
where the ground is dry.

WHITE-TAILED DEER

WHITE IBISES

Willie and Isabella have gone deep into the swamp.
They see six white ibises sitting in the top of a tree.
Ibises usually rest together in large groups called colonies.
Many birds live in the swamp and raise their young there.

Willie asks, "What's the gray stuff hanging all over the trees?"
Johnny tells them it is a plant called Spanish moss.
Do you think it makes the swamp look spooky?

GREAT EGRET CHICKS

Baby egrets have feet that
seem too large for their bodies.
But the chicks will grow
into graceful white birds.
The grown egret in the grass
has just caught a frog.

Two sandhill cranes are wading
in the swamp, looking for food.
Once they looked just like
the fluffy, golden chick.

FLORIDA SANDHILL
CRANES
AND CHICK

GREAT EGRET

GRASSHOPPER

Isabella is trying to push the boat with Johnny's pole.
"It's harder than it looks," Isabella says.
"The bottom feels squishy, and the pole keeps slipping."
The children discover that smooth water makes
a good mirror. A grasshopper catches a free ride.

Isabella and Willie are glad to walk for a while. They can look at the swamp from a walkway built over the watery land.

A sign warns them that bears live here, too.

A black bear splashes through the water, looking for berries. Bears are the largest land animals in the swamp. When they stand up, some bears are taller than a grown man.

AMERICAN BLACK BEAR

19

The children visit
a nature center
to learn more
about the animals in the swamp.
First they pat a young skunk.
Then Isabella makes friends
with a harmless gray rat snake.
The snake stays quietly
in her arms while she pets it.

STRIPED SKUNK

RAT SNAKE

Isabella and Willie are looking at an alligator.
But they don't get too close.
Alligators sometimes swim into the nature center and lie on the grass.
Alligators look lazy lying in the sun, but they can run very fast.

20

WHITE WATER LILY

Johnny tells the children many secrets of the swamp. The water lily will close its petals at night. And the cypress trees grow long roots under the water. When the boat scrapes against the hidden roots, it makes a spooky noise.

HOODED PITCHER PLANTS

The pitcher plant feeds on insects.
Insects crawl down into the leaves
because they have a sweet smell.
Johnny has broken open a leaf.
Can you see the insects inside?

The sundew plant feeds on insects, too.
Red hairs on its leaves have
little drops that are very sticky.
When the fly and the stinkbug landed
on the plant, they got stuck
and could not fly away.
The swamp is full of bright flowers.
A firefly rests on some goldenrod.
Two wasps have landed on a branch
and are looking for nectar in the blossoms.

FIREFLY ON GOLDENROD

FLY AND STINKBUG ON SUNDEW

VICEROY
BUTTERFLY

A butterfly is sipping nectar
from a flower. It can smell food
with two antennae on top of its head.

ave you ever washed your hands with leaves?
Johnny has given the children small, green leaves from a soap bush.
When they rub the leaves with water, it makes real suds.
Willie and Isabella are surprised that it gets their hands clean too!

Johnny has another swamp secret to show the children.
He picks some seeds from the paint-root plant and crushes them.
Indians used the bright orange dye from this plant to paint their faces.
"Let's put some on us!" cries Willie.

GRAY SQUIRREL

During the day, many animals come out of their hiding places.
A bobcat prowls through the swamp, hunting for small animals to eat.
The gray squirrel peeks out from behind a tree.
If it sees danger, it will chatter loudly and shake its bushy tail.
The marsh rabbit escapes its enemies by running away.
Or it may jump in the water and swim to safety.

MARSH RABBIT

As the day ends, the children hear an owl hooting.
It stares out of the shadows with its bright yellow eyes.
A chorus of frogs fills the air with clicks and chirps and squeaks.
Night creatures are taking over the swamp.

The shadows of trees begin to look like strange animals.
The children shine their flashlights into the shadows.
"The swamp must be really spooky at night," Isabella says.
"I wouldn't like to be here by myself," adds Willie.
They are going home, tired but happy. They have seen and heard
things they will remember for a long time. Johnny is happy, too.
He has helped Isabella and Willie explore the swamp.

Published by The National Geographic Society
Robert E. Doyle, *President;* Melvin M. Payne, *Chairman of the Board*
Gilbert M. Grosvenor, *Editor;* Melville Bell Grosvenor, *Editor Emeritus*

Prepared by The Special Publications Division
Robert L. Breeden, *Editor;* Donald J. Crump, *Associate Editor*
Philip B. Silcott, *Senior Editor;* Cynthia Russ Ramsay, *Managing Editor*
Carolyn Leopold Michaels, *Researcher;* Wendy G. Rogers, *Communications Research Assistant*

Illustrations: Don A. Sparks, *Picture Editor;* Jody Bolt, *Art Director*

Production and Printing: Robert W. Messer, *Production Manager;* George V. White, *Assistant Production Manager*
Raja D. Murshed, June L. Graham, Christine A. Roberts, David V. Showers, *Production Assistants*
Debra A. Antonini, Barbara Bricks, Jane H. Buxton, Rosamund Garner, Suzanne J. Jacobson, Katheryn M. Slocum, Suzanne Venino, *Staff Assistants*

Consultants: Dr. Glenn O. Blough, Peter L. Munroe, *Educational Consultants;* Edith K. Chasnov, *Reading Consultant*
Okefenokee National Wildlife Refuge, Dr. Arthur D. Cohen, University of South Carolina, *Scientific Consultants*
The National Geographic Society thanks the staff of the Okefenokee Swamp Park, Waycross, Georgia, for their assistance.

Illustrations Credits: All photographs by Joseph H. Bailey, National Geographic Photographer, except: Wendy W. Cortesi, National Geographic Staff (1, 28 top); Patricia Caulfield, Photo Researchers, Inc. (6, 8 right, 9, 22, 24-25); Wendell D. Metzen (6-7, 10-11, 14 top, 14-15, 15, 19 right, 28 bottom, 29, 32); Leonard Lee Rue III, Photo Researchers, Inc. (8-9); Kelly Dean, Photo Researchers, Inc. (12, 14 bottom); Patricia Caulfield (30). Endpaper painting by Jerry Pinkney

Library of Congress CIP Data   Cortesi, Wendy W., 1941-   Explore a spooky swamp.   (Books for young explorers)
SUMMARY: Two youngsters discover the varied plants and animals that make their home in the watery world of the swamp.
1. Swamp ecology—Juvenile literature. [1. Swamp ecology. 2. Ecology] I. Bailey, Joseph H. II. Title. III. Series.
QH541.5.S9C67   574.5′2632   77-95414   ISBN 0-87044-263-5

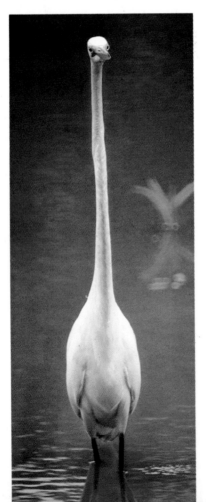

An egret wades
through the swamp
on its long legs.